Pebble® Plus

Endangered and Threatened Animals

by Abbie Dunne

raintree
a Capstone company — publishers for children

Raintree is an imprint of Capstone Global Library Limited, a company incorporated in England and Wales having its registered office at 264 Banbury Road, Oxford, OX2 7DY – Registered company number: 6695582

www.raintree.co.uk
myorders@raintree.co.uk

Text © Capstone Global Library Limited 2017
The moral rights of the proprietor have been asserted.

Edited by Linda Staniford
Designed by Bobbie Nuytten
Picture research by Jo Miller
Production by Tori Abraham

ISBN 978 1 474 72254 4
20 19 18 17 16
10 9 8 7 6 5 4 3 2 1

British Library Cataloguing in Publication Data
A full catalogue record for this book is available from the British Library.

Acknowledgements
We would like to thank the following for permission to reproduce photographs: Capstone Studio: Karon Dubke, 21; Dreamstime: Vishwa Kiran, 17; Newscom: Design Pics/Dave Fleetham, 19; Minden Pictures/FLPA/Michael Gore, 11; Shutterstock: Alexandra Giese, 5, Amy Nichole Harris, 13, hans engbers, 7, Karel Gallas, cover, Matt Gibson, 1, Prezoom.nl, 15, tristan tan, 9

Design Elements
Shutterstock: Alena P

Printed and bound in China.

Contents

Threatened, endangered and extinct

Many animals in our world are thriving. But some are threatened or endangered. Threatened animals could soon be endangered. Endangered animals are close to dying out.

If all of one kind of animal
dies, that animal is extinct.
Dinosaurs are extinct.
There are no longer any
dinosaurs living on Earth.

Habitats

A habitat is where an animal lives. Habitat loss or damage is hard on animals. Trees in rainforests are being cut down. The orangutans who live there are endangered.

People damage animal habitats.

Oil polluted sea otter habitat

in Alaska. Many otters died.

Now sea otters are endangered.

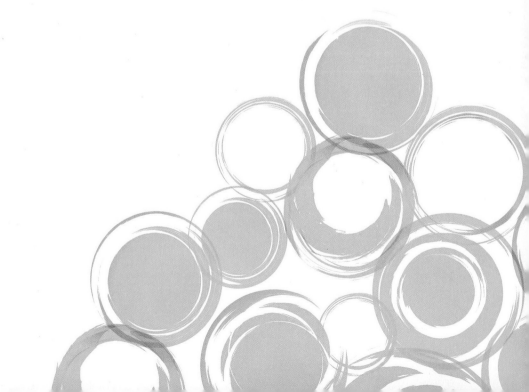

Hunting

Some people hunt animals for food or fur. Too much hunting can endanger animals. People hunt rhinoceroses for their horns. Now rhinos are endangered.

13

Some people catch wild animals to sell as pets. Many great green macaws have been caught. Now they are endangered in the wild.

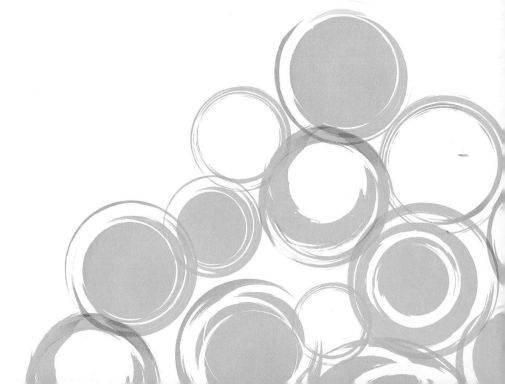

Saving endangered animals

Parks and reserves protect animals. Without them, some animals would die out. Gir National Park in India protects endangered Asiatic lions.

Scientists study animals in their habitats. They try to find out why the animals are endangered. They can help some animals survive.

Activity

A model is a small copy of something. It helps us see things we may not be able to easily spot. Make a model to show how animals can become extinct. Use the chart below.

ANIMAL	ENDANGERED	THREATENED	NO CONCERN
anhinga			X
black vulture			X
blue jay			X
cardinal			X
piping plover		X	
scrub jay		X	
snail kite	X		
wild turkey			X
wood stork	X		
wood warbler	X		

What you need

- pencil
- strips of paper
- box

What you do

1. Write the name of each bird of no concern on six strips of paper.

2. Write the name of each bird that is threatened on two strips of paper.

3. Write the name of each bird that is endangered on one strip of paper.

4. Put all the strips in a box. Mix them up. Draw 20 strips of paper out of the box. These birds are in a new habitat that does not meet their needs. They do not survive.

5. Look in the box to see if any birds became extinct or are very close to becoming extinct.

What do you think?

Make a claim.

A claim is something you believe to be true.

What kind of event can lead animals to become extinct?

Use your model to support your claim.

Glossary

endangered in danger of dying out

extinct no longer living; an extinct animal is one that has died out, with no more of its kind

habitat natural place and conditions where a plant or animal lives

pollute make something dirty or unsafe

rainforest thick forest where rain falls nearly every day

reserve land that is protected so that animals may live there safely

survive stay alive

threatened in danger of becoming endangered

thrive live easily and well

Find out more

Books

Animals in Danger in Africa (Animals in Danger), Richard and Louise Spilsbury (Raintree, 2013)

Disappearing Acts: A Look-and-Find Book of Endangered Animals, Isabella Bunnell (Cicada Publishing Limited, 2016)

The Big Countdown: Ten Thousand, Eight Hundred and Twenty Endangered Species in the Animal Kingdom (Count Down Your World with Infographics), Paul Rockett (Franklin Watts, 2014)

Websites

news.bbc.co.uk/cbbcnews/hi/find_out/guides/animals/endangered_animals_world/newsid_1614000/1614414.stm

Read about endangered animals and what we can do to save them.

http://www.fun-facts.org.uk/animals/animals-endangered.htm

This site has fun facts about endangered animals.

http://www.oum.ox.ac.uk/thezone/animals/extinct/

Read about some extinct animals at the Oxford Universty Museum of Natural History website.

Comprehension questions

1. What is a habitat?

2. Dinosaurs are extinct. Explain what extinct means.

3. Hunting is one way animals can become endangered. Can you name two other ways?

4. Why do you think parks and reserves help save endangered animals?

Index